Tuck T tabs
behind neck

Do not cut out
white area between
arm and body

DOLL A

DOLL B

Ginger Rogers and Fred Astaire
Follow the Fleet (1935)
"Let Yourself Go"

PLATE 1

GK

VE

VE

Tuck T tabs
behind shoulders

Gene Kelly and Vera-Ellen
Words and Music (1948)
"Slaughter on Tenth Avenue"

PLATE 16

Tuck T tab
behind neck

Glue ends of strip
to back of head

Do not cut out
enclosed white area
between arm and body

Gene Kelly and Cyd Charisse
Brigadoon (1954)
"The Heather on the Hill"

PLATE 15

Use face from
Plate 13

Do not cut out
enclosed white
areas between arm
and body.

GK

JG

Gene Kelly and Judy Garland
The Pirate (1948)
"Voodoo"

PLATE 14

GK

JG

JG

Tuck T tab
behind neck

Gene Kelly and Judy Garland
For Me and My Gal (1942)
"For Me and My Gal"

PLATE 13

Tuck T tab
behind face

GK

T

LC

LC

LC

DOLL E

DOLL F

Gene Kelly and Leslie Caron
An American in Paris (1951)
"The Final Ballet"

PLATE 12

GC

Cut slit on dotted line

GC

Tuck T tabs
behind face

T T

Do not cut out white
spaces between arm
and body

MC

Marge and Gower Champion
Show Boat (1951)
"Life Upon the Wicked Stage"

PLATE 11

DOLL C

DOLL D

Marge and Gower Champion
Jupiter's Darling (1955)
"The Life of an Elephant"

PLATE 10

Tuck T tab behind
shoulder

Glue ends of strip
to back of head

Do not cut out
white area between
arm and body

Vera-Ellen
Three Little Words (1950)
"Nevertheless"

Cyd Charisse
The Band Wagon (1953)
"The Girl Hunt"

PLATE 9

Do not cut out
enclosed white
area between arm
and body

Ginger Rogers and Fred Astaire
The Barkleys of Broadway (1949)
"My Highland Fling"

PLATE 8

Glue dark edges
to back of head

Leave bottom
edge open

Judy Garland and Fred Astaire
Easter Parade (1948)
"We're a Couple of Swells"

PLATE 7

Fred Astaire
Generic costume with tie belt

Fred Astaire
The Band Wagon (1953)
"The Girl Hunt"

PLATE 6

Tuck T tabs behind
shoulders

Do not cut out
white area between
arm and body

Rita Hayworth
You'll Never Get Rich (1941)
"So Near and Yet So Far"

Rita Hayworth
You Were Never Lovelier (1942)
"You Were Never Lovelier"

PLATE 5

Tuck T tab
behind face

Do not cut out
white area between
arm and body

GR

T

GR

Ginger Rogers
Shall We Dance (1937)
"They All Laughed"

Ginger Rogers
The Story of Vernon and Irene Castle (1938)
"The Castle Walk"

PLATE 4

Tuck T tab
behind face

Do not cut out
white area between
arm and body

GR

GR

GR

Ginger Rogers
Top Hat (1935)
"Dancing Cheek to Cheek"

Ginger Rogers
The Gay Divorcee (1934)
"The Continental"

PLATE 3

Do not cut out
white area between
arm and body

Ginger Rogers and Fred Astaire
Follow the Fleet (1935)
"Let's Face the Music and Dance"

PLATE 2